APPLES A to Z

words by **Margaret McNamara**
pictures by **Jake Parker**

Scholastic Press
New York

All rights reserved. Published by Scholastic Press, an imprint of Scholastic Inc., *Publishers since 1920.*
SCHOLASTIC, SCHOLASTIC PRESS, and associated logos are trademarks and/or registered trademarks of Scholastic Inc.

Library of Congress Cataloging-in-Publication Data
McNamara, Margaret.
Apples A to Z / by Margaret McNamara; pictures by Jake Parker. — 1st ed.
p. cm.
Includes bibliographical references and index.
ISBN 978-0-439-72808-9 (alk. paper) — ISBN 978-0-439-72809-6 (alk. paper). 1. Apples—Juvenile literature.
2. English language—Alphabet— Juvenile literature. I. Parker, Jake, 1977— ill. II. Title.
SB363.M395 2012
634'.11—dc22
2010045432
10 9 8 7 6 5 4 3 2 1   12 13 14 15 16

Printed in Singapore 46
First edition, August 2012

The display type was set in CircusMouse.
The text was set in 18-point MartinGothic.
Book design by Phil Falco

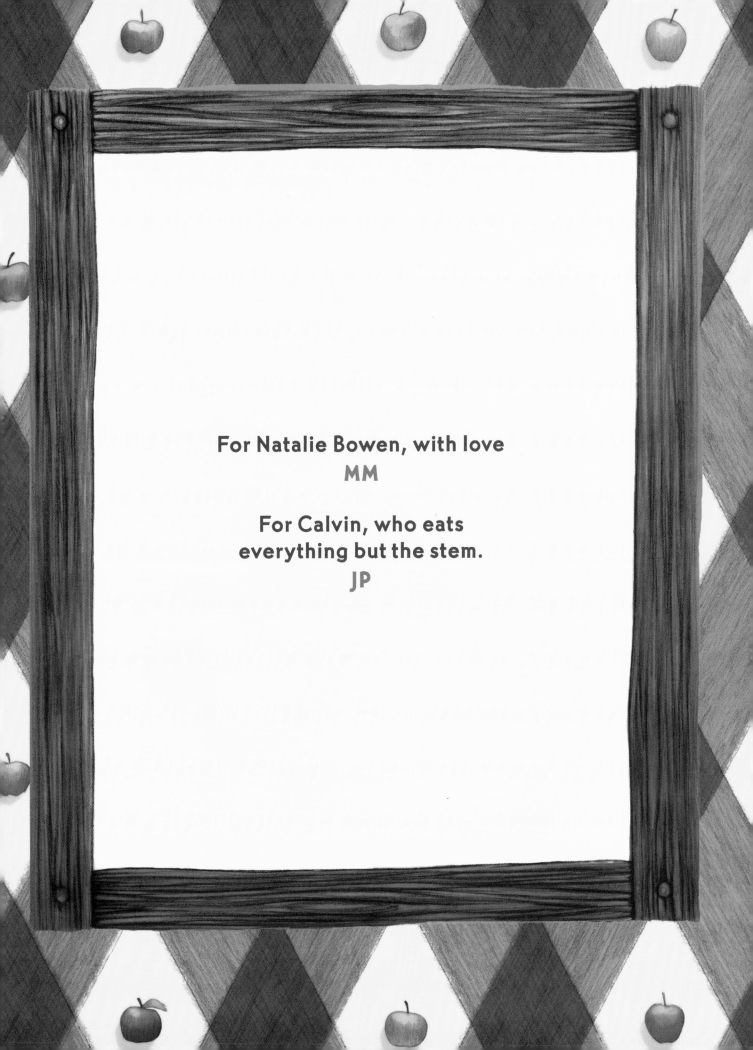

For Natalie Bowen, with love
MM

For Calvin, who eats
everything but the stem.
JP

A is for APPLES

Fox loves apples. Apples are one of the most popular fruits in the world. Every year, about 68 million tons of apples are harvested.

B is for BLOSSOMS

By late spring, apple trees are covered in blossoms, or flowers. When the blossoms fall off the trees' branches, the fruits begin to form.

C is for CIDER

Bear makes cider by pressing apples —
skins, seeds, and all — into a cloudy, pulpy
juice. Cider can be served hot or cold.

D is for DECIDUOUS

Apple trees lose their leaves in the fall.
This makes them deciduous trees.

E is for EATING

Fox and his friends eat raw apples, cooked apples, and dried apples. Delicious!

F is for FRUIT

An apple is a kind of fruit. Some other fruits are oranges, bananas, and grapes. Fruits contain seeds and come from flowering plants.

G is for GRAFTING

Fox attaches a branch of one kind of apple tree to a branch of another. This is called grafting. It can produce stronger, healthier trees, and tastier apples.

H is for HARVEST

Fall is harvest time, when ripe apples are picked
from the trees. Apple picking is more fun with friends.

I is for **ICE**

Apple trees are very hardy, but winter ice storms can break branches and keep fruit from growing in the spring.

J is for JUICE

Apple juice, like cider, is pressed from apples,
but apple juice is filtered to be clear.

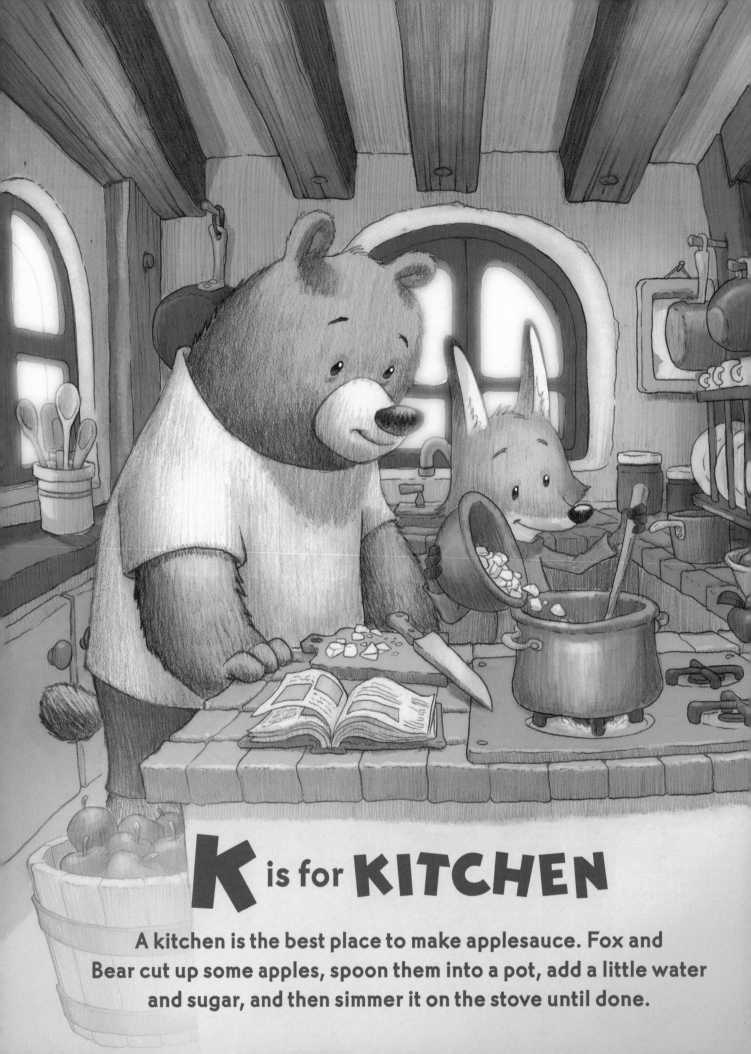

K is for KITCHEN

A kitchen is the best place to make applesauce. Fox and Bear cut up some apples, spoon them into a pot, add a little water and sugar, and then simmer it on the stove until done.

L is for LEAVES

Apple leaves are oval shaped, with small points.
The edges of the leaves are "toothed."

M is for **MARKETS**

Farmers' markets and grocery stores are filled with many varieties of apples. Fox looks for Granny Smith, one of his favorite kinds of apples.

N is for NUTRITIOUS

Apples are a very healthy, natural food. They have
no fat, and they contain fiber, which helps your stomach
digest other foods.

O is for ORCHARD

An apple orchard is an apple farm. Apples are grown in every state in the United States and in every province in Canada.

P is for POLLEN

Pollen from apple blossoms makes it possible for an apple fruit to form inside the flower. Bees help move pollen from one apple blossom to another.

Q is for QUARTERS

Fox cuts his apple into quarters — four pieces of the same size. How many quarters make a half?

R is for RIPE

A ripe red apple is . . . irresistible!
The codling moth caterpillar likes
eating them as much as Fox does.

S is for SEEDS

Fox cuts an apple in half. In the center is a star shape with five points, and each point of the star contains a seed.

T is for TREES

All apples grow on trees. Some apple trees can grow
to be one hundred years old.

U is for UNDERGROUND

The roots of an apple tree spread underground. Roots soak up water and nutrients and keep the tree from falling down.

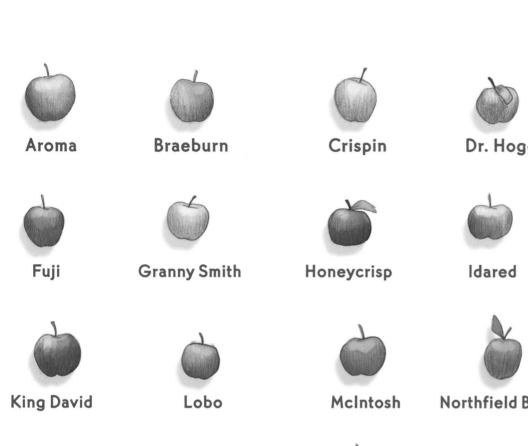

Aroma

Braeburn

Crispin

Dr. Hogg

Empire

Fuji

Granny Smith

Honeycrisp

Idared

Jeffries

King David

Lobo

McIntosh

Northfield Beauty

Oriole

Pinova

Queen Cox

Red Delicious

Seek-no-further

Topaz

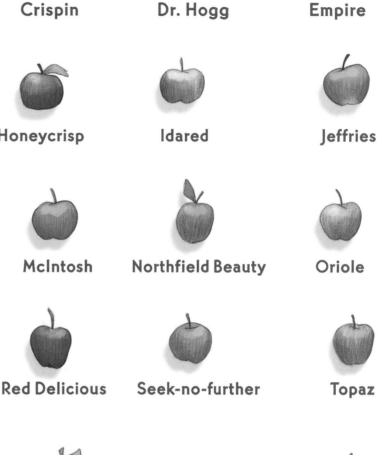

Ultrared Gala

Viking

Winesap

Xavier de Bavay

York

Zabergau

V is for VARIETIES

There are hundreds of varieties of apples. Each variety looks and tastes different. Try them all!

 is for **WAX**

Fox rubbed an apple on his shirt, polishing the natural wax on the apple's skin. The wax helps keep the apple from drying out.

X is for an X in an APPLE PIE

It's as easy as pie to make an apple pie. And rolling out the dough is a lot of fun. Cut an X in the top of the pie dough to let steam escape while the pie bakes.

Y is for YIELD

One tree can produce hundreds of apples.
The apples collected from a tree are called its yield.

Z is for ZERO

Fox ate the last apple. Now there are zero apples left!

APPLE ACTIVITIES

All these activities need the help of a grown-up.

VISIT AN ORCHARD

Find an orchard and pick your own apples. There are many resources online that will help you locate orchards near you.

CREATE APPLE PRINTS

Cut an apple in half. Press the apple half into an ink pad or paint. Then press the apple half onto paper to make apple prints.

MAKE EASY CHUNKY APPLESAUCE

8 — 12 apples (the best varieties to use for this recipe are fresh picked Jonagold, Pink Lady, or Macoun), cored and cut into chunks. No need to peel!

1/4 cup sugar
1 pinch salt
1 cup water

Stir all the ingredients together in a large, heavy saucepan. Cover the pot and cook over medium-high heat for about 15 to 20 minutes. Stir with a wooden spoon as the apples are cooking. At the end of the cooking time, mash the apples against the side of the pot to get them to the right consistency. Serve warm or at room temperature. (Makes about 3 cups)

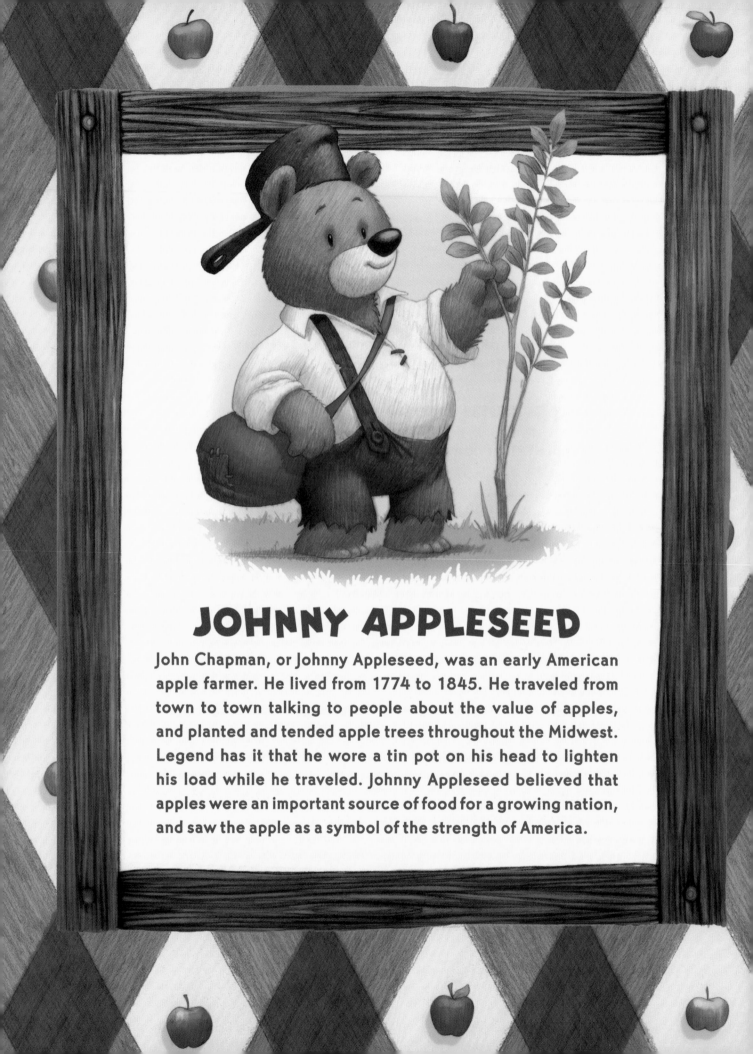

JOHNNY APPLESEED

John Chapman, or Johnny Appleseed, was an early American apple farmer. He lived from 1774 to 1845. He traveled from town to town talking to people about the value of apples, and planted and tended apple trees throughout the Midwest. Legend has it that he wore a tin pot on his head to lighten his load while he traveled. Johnny Appleseed believed that apples were an important source of food for a growing nation, and saw the apple as a symbol of the strength of America.

APPLE FUN

There are a lot of common expressions that use the word *apple*. Here are a few of them, along with their meanings:

An apple a day keeps the doctor away. Apples are healthy! An apple a day won't really keep you from ever getting sick, but it will provide your body with natural vitamins and minerals.

The apple of my eye. This is an expression that means "beloved." The apple of your eye is someone you love very much.

The Big Apple. This is a nickname for New York City.

As American as apple pie. Apple trees were planted by the earliest Americans, and people in this country have been enjoying apple pies ever since. Apple pie is one of America's most popular desserts (especially when it's topped with vanilla ice cream!).

A bad apple. This is an expression that refers to a person who is a bad influence on other people. It comes from the fact that one bad apple in a barrel quickly makes other apples around it rotten, too.

How do you like them apples? This is slang for "So there!"

An apple for the teacher. An apple is a gift traditionally given to a teacher as a token of thanks.

JUST JOKING

What lives in an apple and loves to read? *A bookworm!*

What did one apple say to another apple? *You're a saucy one!*

What kind of apple has a bad temper? *A crab apple!*

Why did the apple go out with a fig? *Because it couldn't find a date!*

What kind of an apple isn't an apple? *A pineapple!*

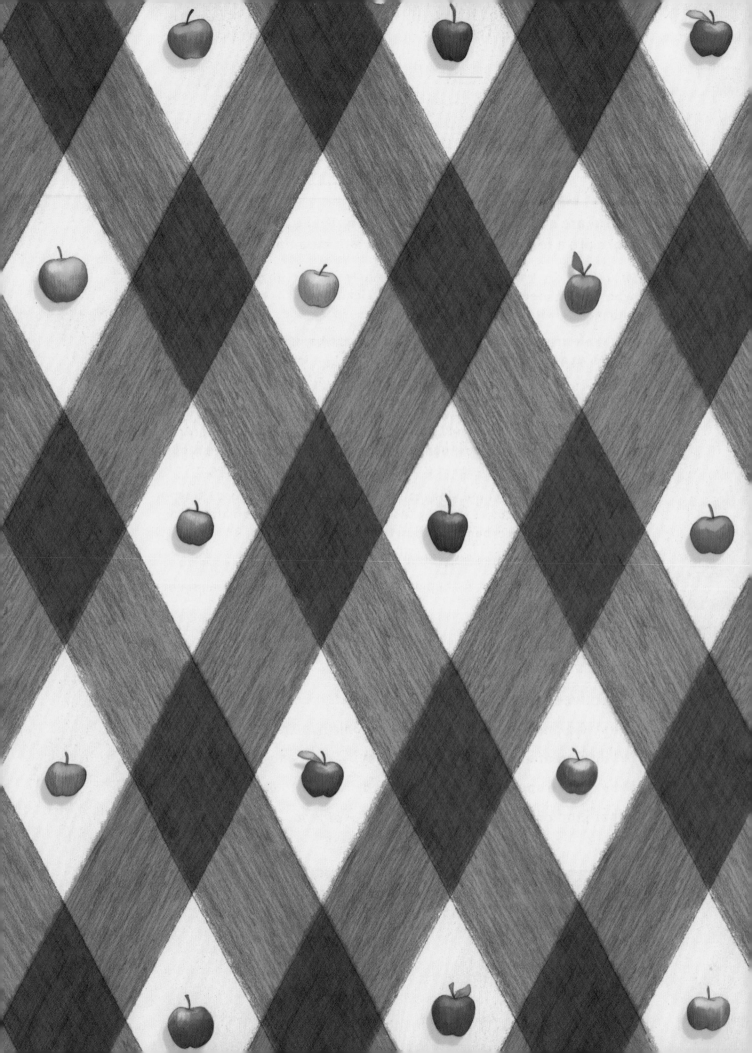